Fun Crafts with
Dots and
Lines

Enslow Elementary
an imprint of
E **Enslow Publishers, Inc.**
40 Industrial Road   PO Box 38
Box 398   Aldershot
Berkeley Heights, NJ 07922   Hants GU12 6BP
USA   UK
http://www.enslow.com

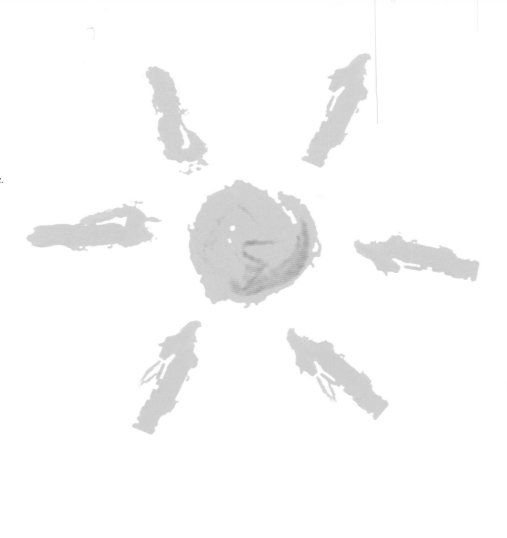

Enslow Elementary, an imprint of Enslow Publishers, Inc.

Enslow Elementary® is a registered trademark of Enslow Publishers, Inc.

Translated from the Spanish edition by Toby S. McLellan, edited by
Susana C. Schultz, of Strictly Spanish, LLC. Edited and produced by
Enslow Publishers, Inc.

Library-in-Cataloging Publication Data

Ros, Jordina.
  [Punto y la linea. English]
  Fun crafts with dots and lines / Jordina Ros, Pere Estadella.
     p. cm. — (Arts and crafts fun)
  Originally published: Barcelona, Spain : Parramón, c2003.
  ISBN 0-7660-2656-6
  1. Art—Technique—Juvenile literature. 2. Dots (Art)—Juvenile literature.
3. Line (Art)—Juvenile literature. 4. Handicraft—Juvenile literature.
I. Estadella, Pere. II. Title. III. Series.
  N7440.R677513 2005
  701'.8—dc22
                        2005011220

Originally published in Spanish under the title *El punto y la línea.*
Copyright © 2003 PARRAMÓN EDICIONES, S.A., - World Rights.
Published by Parramón Ediciones, S.A., Barcelona, Spain.
Spanish edition produced by: Parramón Ediciones, S.A.
Authors: Jordina Ros and Pere Estadella
Collection and scale model design: Comando gráfico, S.L.
Photography: Estudio Nos & Soto, Jordina Ros, René Martin, Corel
© the authorized reproductions, VEGAP, Barcelona
Parramón Ediciones, S.A., would like to give special thanks to Pol, Irene,
Luisa, and María, who did such a wonderful job posing for the
photographs in this book.

Printed in Spain

10 9 8 7 6 5 4 3 2 1

Fun Crafts with Dots and Lines

Table of Contents

Things to Remember . . .

Make sure you have everything you need!
Before you start the craft, go over the list of materials.

Be careful with sharp objects!
You may be using sharp tools, such as scissors or something to punch holes with. Always ask an adult for permission or for help!

Imagination
If you come up with a new idea while working on these crafts, tell a teacher or another adult. Together you can create new crafts that are all your own.

What Is a Dot?

**The impact of any type of tool
on a surface can make a dot.**

*A dot is the simplest form
of artistic expression!*

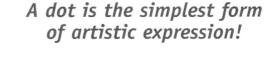

You can make a dot with a hole puncher, the tip of a paintbrush, or a pencil point. You can make a dot on a piece of paper or any other surface. You can even make a dot with a piece of clay!

You can also group dots of different sizes, shapes, and colors in the same space. This is a fun way to fill in shapes!

How Big Is a Dot?

*This drawing
is full of drops
of water.*

*The shapes of the
raindrops are dots.*

Dots don't have to be tiny. They can be any size—as long as they are round!

• You can make a big dot by cutting or tearing a piece of newspaper and pasting it onto your artwork.

• To make a medium-sized dot, wet the tip of your index finger with paint and press it in the center of a piece of paper.

• If you want to make a small dot, you can press the point of a fine-tipped marker onto your paper.

If you make a handprint, you will see that each one of your fingertips has many dots of different sizes: large, medium, and small.

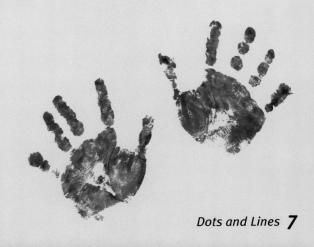

Dots and Spots

How is a dot different from a spot?

Dots are round. They may be filled with color or just be a round outline—in other words, a circle!

Spots can be any shape. They can be round or completely irregular.

If you use a small paintbrush to splash or splatter paint onto a piece of paper, you will probably end up with lots of dots—and lots of spots!

Use a ring or a little hoop to help you draw a nice circle!

You can put dots and spots on an old T-shirt—just make sure to get permission first!

Dots and Spots All Around Us

If you pay attention, you can find dots and spots all around you.

These flowers look like white spots with yellow dots in the middle!

This orange ball in the yard is a dot.

You could use white dots and spots to paint these stars.

From up here, those people look like little dots!

Lots of Dots!

What you will need...
Clay
Roller
Cup or large glass
Paintbrush
Glue stick
Glitter (various colors)

Protect your work surface with a piece of plastic or a floor tile.

Use a roller to model the clay into a sheet about 1/4 inch thick.

Place the mouth of the cup over the clay. Press it down and separate the clay from the sides. Now you should have a circle—a big dot!

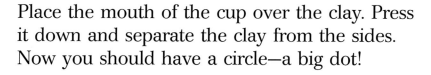

Use the handle of the paintbrush to press some medium-sized "dots" into the clay disk.

Wait for the clay to dry, then continue decorating.

Spread glue over the clay disk and sprinkle on the colored glitter—now you have tiny dots!

This clay "cookie" is just a bunch of dots—a big dot of clay, medium dots from the paintbrush, and tiny dots of glitter!

YOU CAN TRY
Start with another big dot of clay. What other things can you make with it, using only dots?

A Funny Clown

What you will need
White poster board
Yellow and orange finger paints
Fine-tipped paintbrush
Blue marker
Round blue and red stickers
Yellow, green, orange, red, light blue,
   and dark blue shiny paper.
Glue stick
Tracing paper
Pencil
Pattern (page 46)

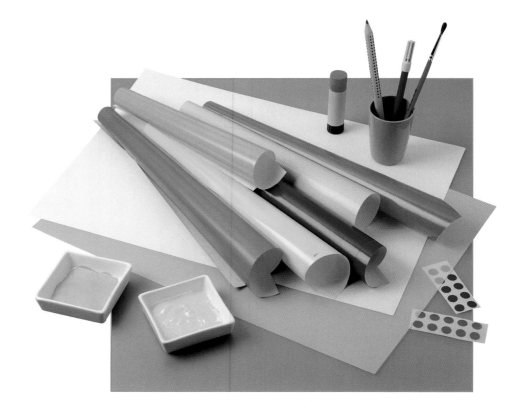

Do you like clowns?

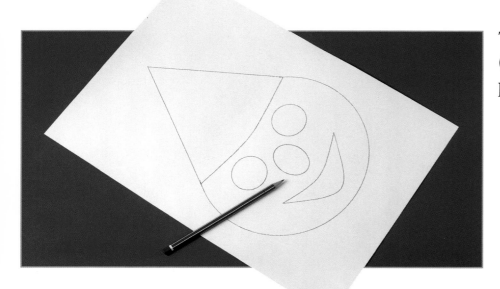

Trace the clown pattern
(page 46) onto the white
poster board.

*So far this clown is very boring.
Let's fill it in with some
crazy dots and spots!*

Use your finger to cover the whole surface of the clown's face with dots of yellow paint.

Fill in the nose with round red stickers.

Use the paintbrush to fill in the mouth with dots of orange paint.

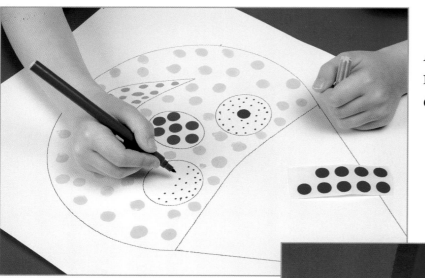

Add small dots to the eyes with a blue marker. Put a blue sticker in the middle of each eye.

How about using square spots to fill in the hat?

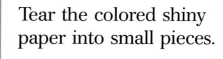

Tear the colored shiny paper into small pieces.

Glue them inside the clown's hat.

Now that's a very funny clown!

YOU CAN TRY
Try making a whole circus using dots and spots!

The Starry Sky

What you will need...

White poster board
White construction paper
Dark blue, white, and yellow finger paints
Sponge
Fine-tipped paintbrush
Hole puncher or scissors
Pencil
Glue stick
Pattern (page 47)

Do you want to paint a sky full of stars?

Wet a piece of sponge in the dark blue paint. Start stamping dots and spots on the white poster board. Don't fill it all in.

Mix a little white paint in with the dark blue paint. Use another piece of sponge to finish covering the poster board.

Now you have a beautiful blue sky! Wash your hands while it dries.

Now for the stars...

Trace stars from the pattern (page 47) onto the white construction paper. Make as many as you like!

Paint the inside of the stars with yellow dots.

These will really twinkle!

Let the stars dry, then punch or cut them out from the paper.

Scatter and glue the stars all around your sky.

What a bright, starry night!
Now you can have a small piece
of the sky in your room.

YOU CAN TRY
Try making a sunny sky to go with your
starry sky. What would you do differently?

Frame It!

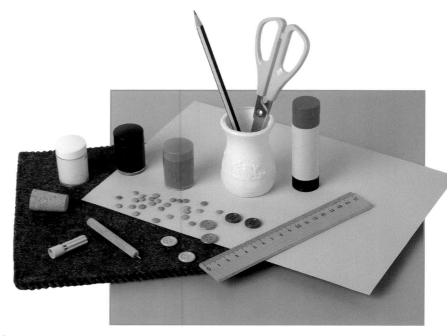

What you will need...

Plain poster board
Medium-sized buttons (various colors)
Cork stopper
Marker cap
Glue-stick cap
Lentils
Glue stick
Green, black, and white poster paint
Ruler, pencil, and scissors
Hole puncher or scissors

*You will be making
a frame of dots for this craft.*

Draw a 9.5" x 7.5" rectangle on the poster board. Centered inside that, draw a 5.5" x 3.5" rectangle.

Cut out the large rectangle with scissors, then punch or cut out the smaller one.

Glue the lentils and buttons to your frame. Use the marker cap to make outlines of dots with green paint. Use the cork to make dots of black paint.

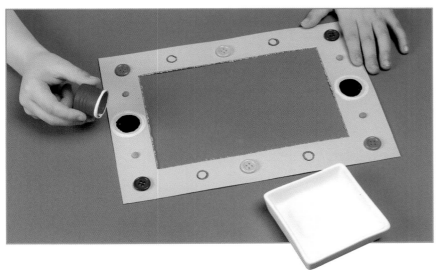

Use the glue-stick cap and white paint to make large empty dots around the black dots.

Frame your favorite drawing and hang it in your room!

TIP
If the glue-stick cap isn't big enough, use a paintbrush to paint the white circles around the black dots.

Still Life with Dots and Spots

What you will need...

Pink poster board
Pink, white, light green, orange, and
 yellow construction paper
Tracing paper
Glue stick
Dark blue, light blue, and white clay
Red, green, and yellow poster paint
Fine-tipped paintbrush
Hole puncher or scissors
Scissors
Pattern (page 48)

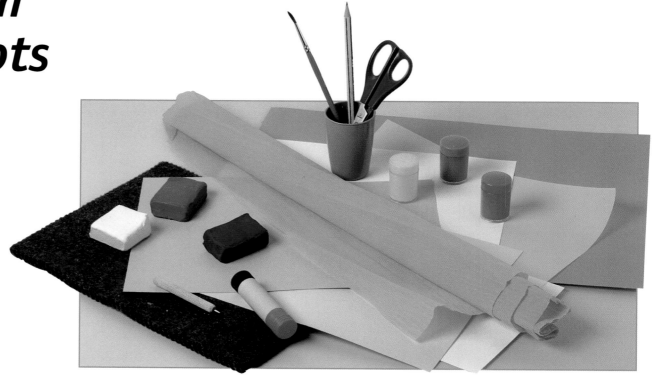

*A still life is a picture of objects
that do not move, such as pottery
or flowers or fruit.*

Cut the pink construction paper
into small pieces. Glue them onto
the pink poster board so that it is
completely covered.

Use the pattern (page 48) to trace the fruit bowl on the white paper, the pear on the green paper, the orange on the orange paper, and the banana on the yellow paper.

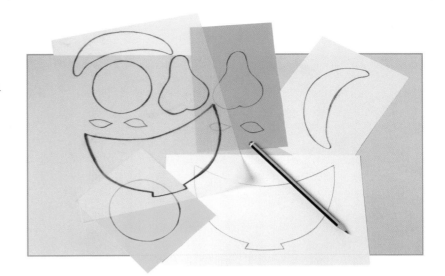

Dot the inside of each fruit with the same color paint. Let them dry, then punch or cut out each shape from the paper.

That was easy—the colors of the fruits are the same as the colors of the paper!

How can you decorate the bowl?

Punch or cut out the fruit bowl. Make white clay balls to decorate the edges of the bowl. Make light and dark blue clay balls to fill in the bowl.

Glue the three dotted fruits in the middle of the pink poster board. Then add on the fruit bowl.

Now you have a real still life!

YOU CAN TRY

Try using different materials to make other still lifes. Can you make one showing flowers in a vase?

"The Red Buoy" by Paul Signac (1863–1935)

Paul Signac was a French painter who lived at the end of the nineteenth century and the beginning of the twentieth century.

He almost always painted with dots of color. He put different colors on his palette. Then he applied them to the canvas with a small paintbrush, without mixing them.

Paul Signac really liked the sea. Many of his paintings feature seascapes and ports. This painting is called *The Red Buoy*. Signac painted it at Saint-Tropez, in France. It must have taken a long time for him to paint all those colored dots!

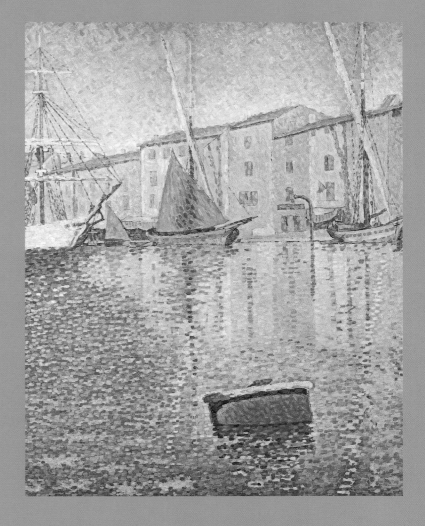

What Is a Line?

You can think of a line as a way of connecting dots! A straight line is the shortest distance between two points.

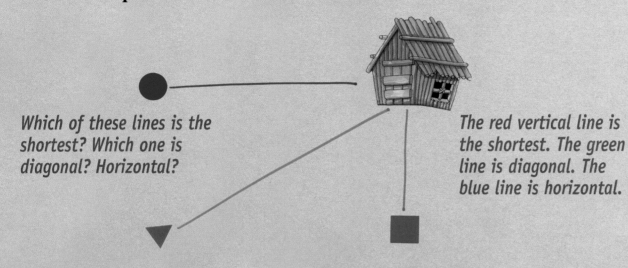

Which of these lines is the shortest? Which one is diagonal? Horizontal?

The red vertical line is the shortest. The green line is diagonal. The blue line is horizontal.

Straight lines can go in any direction. They can be vertical (up and down), horizontal (left to right), or diagonal (at an angle).

There are many different kinds of lines you can make—straight, crossed, wavy, zigzag... You can make some very original compositions just by using lines.

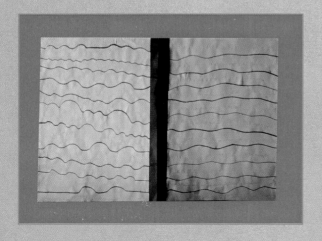

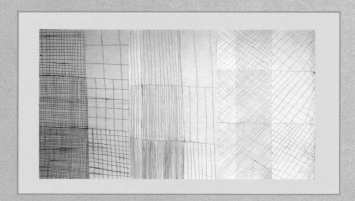

Line Shapes and Sizes

Did you know that the palm of your hand is filled with lines? Just look— I have painted some of the lines on my hand!

You can draw lines with different shapes.

- You would use a very simple stroke to draw a straight line. The stroke for a curve is more complex. The shortest route between two points is a straight line. A curvy line between the same two points would be longer.

- You can make open lines or closed lines. An open line has a beginning and an end. A closed line starts and ends at the same point.

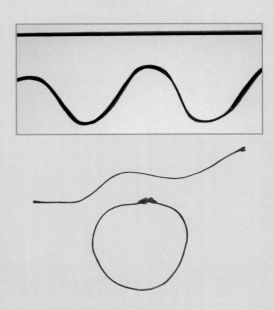

You can draw lines of different sizes.

- You can paint thin lines with a paintbrush, or thick lines with a roller.

- You can draw short lines or long lines. The line you would draw to show the length of the green pencil would be shorter than the line you would need for the yellow pencil.

Lines All Around Us

Look around you. See how easy it is to identify the different types of lines.

Look at this park bench, for example—it has lots of straight lines!

The roofs of houses also have lines.

The trails of these airplanes are white lines that appear in the sky.

The grill on this window also has lines.

The Doodle Line

A doodle is an irregular stroke. It may look like just a scribble to you—but it is a very important stroke! It is the beginning of all the expressions made through drawing, painting, and writing.

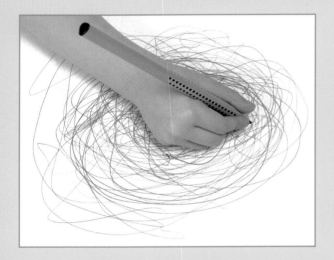

The uncontrolled doodle

This is usually one of the first strokes a child makes. They can be any length, direction, or shape. But you can make an uncontrolled doodle anytime—they're fun to do!

The doodle with a name

As a person's strokes become more certain, they begin to give more form to their drawings. Often they will even add a name or personality to them!

This is someone's mom!

The controlled doodle

As a person's visual and motor skills develop, their strokes become horizontal lines, vertical lines, or dots and circles.

Line Art!

What you will need...

White poster board
Glue stick
Medium-point blue marker
Green and red finger paints
Sewing thread
Spaghetti
Newsprint
Thick paintbrush
Cord
Pencil
Scissors

Can you imagine how many different kinds of lines you can make with these materials?

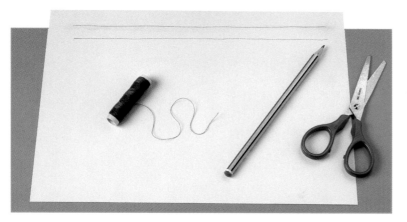

Cut a piece of thread, then glue it onto the poster board. Use a pencil to trace a line of the same length and thickness as the line of thread.

Glue the spaghetti below the pencil line. Then make another straight line beneath it with the medium-point blue marker.

The straightest line so far is probably the spaghetti!

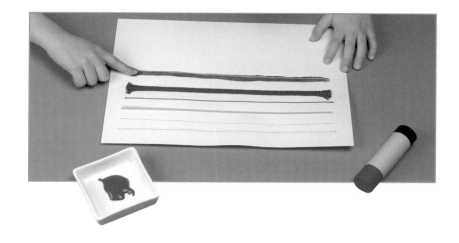

Now glue the cord to the poster board. Use the tip of your finger to paint a straight green line below that.

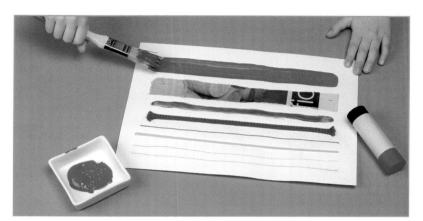

You're not done yet...

Tear a strip of newsprint with your fingers, then glue it to the poster board. Use the thick paintbrush to paint a red line below it.

There are many more lines you could make!

YOU CAN TRY
Try making other kinds of lines. How does it look if you alternate thin lines with thick lines? Or make many thin lines, all with the same color? How about with different colors?

Weaving with Lines

What you will need...

Two sheets of white construction paper
Black poster board
Two paint rollers
Orange and green poster paints
Black crayon
Glue stick

Cover the table with newspapers.
You don't want to get paint all over it!

Use a roller to paint one piece of white construction paper green, and another one orange.

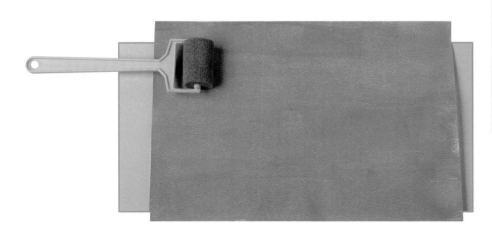

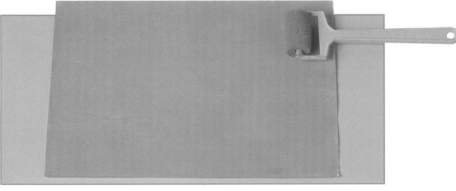

Wait for them to dry...

Once they are dry, tear the orange and green pages to make long strips.

Use the black crayon to draw continuous lines in the middle of the orange strips.

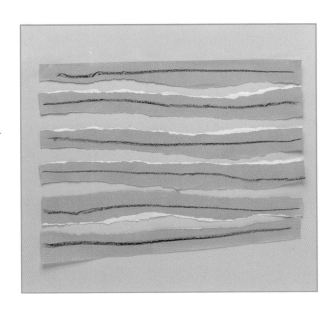

Draw dashed lines in the middle of the green strips.

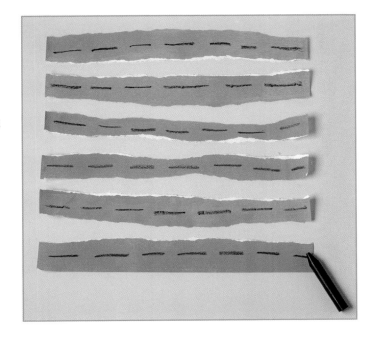

Do you want to experiment with vertical and horizontal lines? Turn the page!

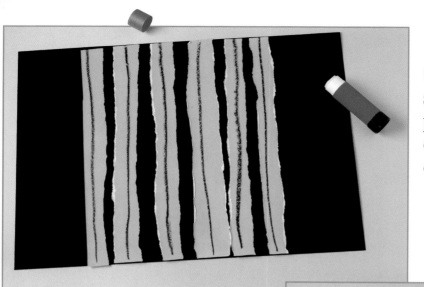

Glue one end of each orange strip to the top of the black poster board. Keep a distance of almost an inch between each of them.

Now glue one end of each green strip to the side of the black poster board.

*Very good—
now you can weave the
horizontal and vertical
strips together!*

Weave the green horizontal strips through the orange vertical strips. When you are finished, glue the other end of each strip to the poster board.

Your woven artwork is a great way to show horizontal and vertical lines!

YOU CAN TRY
Try weaving a set of placemats for your family!
You can use different colors for each person.

Mountains and Waves

What you will need...

White, blue, green, black, and
  yellow corrugated cardboard
Pink poster board
Black and white pencils
Scissors
Glue stick
Tracing paper
Pattern (page 47)

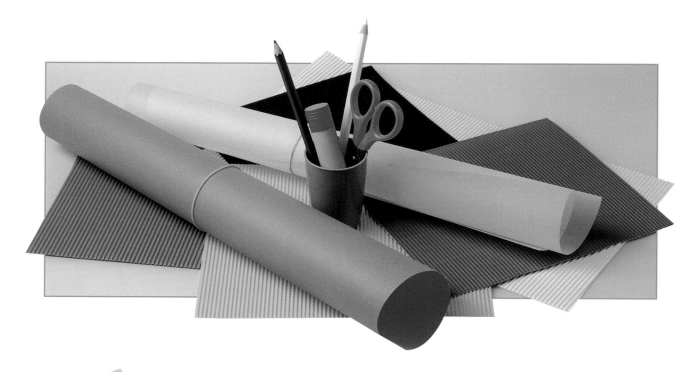

*This craft takes you all the way
from the mountains to the sea!*

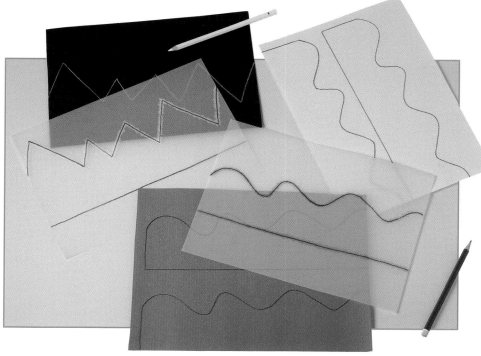

Use the pattern (page 47) to trace the sea
waves onto the white and blue corrugated
cardboard. Trace the mountains onto the
black cardboard.

Cut out the waves and mountains.

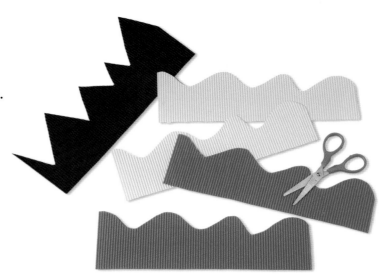

**Which do you prefer,
the sea or the mountains?**

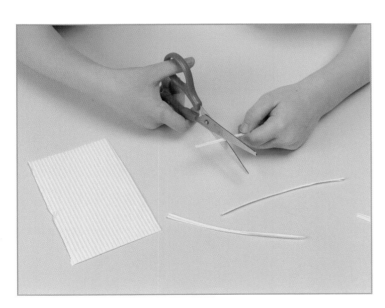

Cut small pieces from the leftover
white cardboard. You will use these
for snow on the mountains.

Also cut green pieces for plants, and
blue and yellow pieces for the sky.

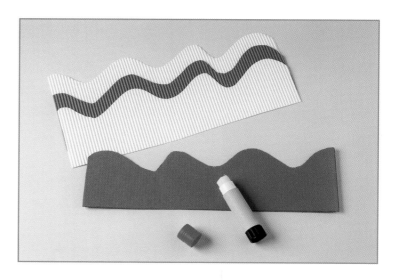

Glue the white and blue waves together, in layers.

Glue the curvy waves and pointy mountains onto the pink poster board. Then glue the strips of snow to the mountains, diagonally.

Glue the blue and yellow lines onto the sky, horizontally. Finish your landscape by gluing the green strips vertically and diagonally along the mountains and the sea.

This landscape includes many different kinds of lines!

TIP

If you can't find all the different colors of cardboard you need for this craft, you can paint plain corrugated cardboard any color you like. If you don't have any cardboard, use construction paper instead.

Magic Doodles

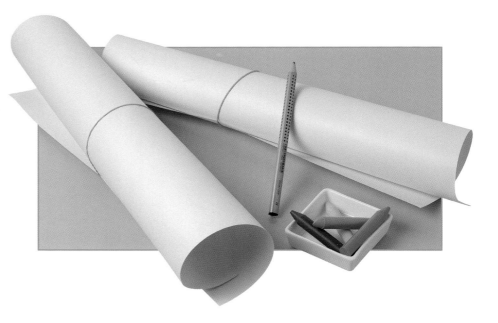

Color one piece of white poster board yellow.

Do you want to have fun doodling?

Over the yellow, color a third of the poster board pink, another third green, and the last third orange.

Place the other poster board on top of the colored one.

Use the pencil to doodle on the white poster board. Press hard!

Lift the poster board and take a look at the other side. It's just like magic!

YOU CAN TRY
Try making a magic drawing this way. Instead of doodling on the clean paper, draw a regular picture—a face, a puppy, or a picture of your favorite place. Remember, it will come out looking backward—so draw it the opposite way from how you want it to look!

Spiral Doodles

You'll be making spirals for this craft. Putting on some fun music while you work will put you in the mood to spin around!

Tear five strips of tissue paper. Each strip should be a different color.

Roll each strip of paper into a ball.

*Listen to the music...
and get swept away!*

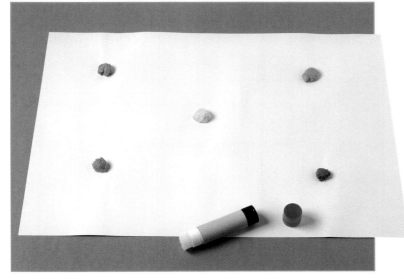

Glue the five balls onto the white poster board. Place one in the center and the others toward the four corners.

Use a marker to make round spiral doodles around one of the balls.

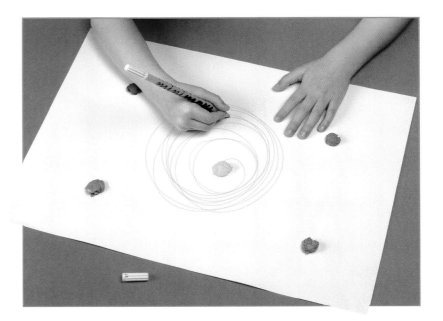

Do the same around the
rest of the balls, using different colors.

*Those are some crazy spirals!
You can make spiral doodles with
crayons, with paint—even in the sand!*

YOU CAN TRY

Try using spiral doodles to make a regular drawing.
You can use orange for the sun, green for the top
of a tree, and different colors for flowers.